Planting Trees
and Sowing Seeds

Valerie!

Thank you for joining
with us in Song.

(Thank you, too, for
sharing Wellington
memories....)

[signature]

Planting Trees and Sowing Seeds

23 new hymns by
FRED KAAN

with a foreword by
BRUCE KENT

For Anthea

Pray that at the end of living,
of philosophies and creeds,
God will find his people busy
planting trees and sowing seeds.

OXFORD UNIVERSITY PRESS

HOPE PUBLISHING COMPANY

Published by
Oxford University Press, Walton Street, Oxford OX2 6DP

Oxford New York Toronto
Delhi Bombay Calcutta Madras Karachi
Petaling Jaya Singapore Hong Kong Tokyo
Nairobi Dar es Salaam Cape Town
Melbourne Auckland

and associated companies in
Berlin Ibadan

Oxford is a trade mark of Oxford University Press

for USA and Canada
Hope Publishing Company, Carol Stream, IL 60188

USA © 1989 Hope Publishing Company
All other parts of the world © Oxford University Press 1989

First printed in 1989

ISBN 0 19 143481 7

Printed in Great Britain by Information Press Ltd.

FOREWORD

I find it hard to write an introduction to Fred Kaan's latest collection of hymns without having Psalm 104 running through my mind:

> I will sing to the Lord all my life,
> make music to my God while I live.

Such singing is the author's great talent. He speaks through hymnody more effectively than most sermons will ever do. Few could fail to recognise his warm, generous, and faithful Christian inspiration.

The themes chosen in this collection are broadly based. There is impatience with the Church, which, as in *A Hymn on Choosing Life*, is urged to 'turn into creative deeds the inner urges of our creeds.' But there is also a great love for that strange community of Christ-seeking people. In *Round-Table Church* it is beautifully described just like that: a table which has 'no sides or corners, no first or last, no honours …'

Here, too, are great moments of compassion. Not everyone would remember that on every Mothering Sunday there will be those present with sad hearts who have never been given the joy of children. So we remember 'those who have no children, yet are parents under God.'

There is something for everyone here. For the bereaved, for the divorced, for those thinking of giving up, and especially for those working for justice and peace, with, and in, and even despite the churches.

A hymn-writer is a sower of seeds. These words with their music will move hearts and minds in gatherings large and small around the world. Fred's work, of which this collection is yet another chapter, will help to draw many to the God of whom the Psalmist, another songwriter, declared long ago:

> The lands of sunrise and sunset
> you fill with your joy. *Psalm 65:8*

Bruce Kent

TOPICAL INDEX

INDEX OF FIRST LINES

1 A TIME-WARP HYMN

KAIROS 64 64 64

John Garside

Be - fore a Word was said, God had our ___ ear;

be - fore the world was made, Je - sus was ___ here.

A - head of A - bra - ham, God was, I am.

Before a Word was said,
God had our ear;
before the world was made,
Jesus was here.
Ahead of Abraham,
God was, I am.

2 Before the Word assumed
our flesh and blood,
Jesus among us roomed
and with us stood.
Ahead of Abraham,
God was, I am.

3 God, Span of future, past,
our present Tense,
your Word is first and last,
eternal Sense.
Ahead of Abraham,
you are, I am.

Fred Kaan

Bread and wine
for two or three,
twelve or thousands,
you and me,
bread and wine
for those who meet as one.

2 Words that are spoken
and bread that is broken,
wine that is tasted
and love that is feasted
lead us to service,
to deeds that are meant and done.

3 Circles for caring
and gestures of sharing;
heaven is near us:
there's laughter to cheer us,
hope to renew us
till fear and despair have gone.

4 We shall be one family,
Christ for all
for two or three,
bread and wine
uniting you and me.

Fred Kaan

3 A HYMN ON CHOOSING LIFE

JOYFUL COMPANY LM   Peter Cutts

Choose life, choose love—the hour is late! Say 'yes' to Christ

_ and 'no' to fate. Join hands with peo-ple of the

faith, reach out in hope____ to all who live.

EISENACH LM

J. H. Schein (1586–1630)

Choose life, choose love – the hour is late! Say
'yes' to Christ and 'no' to fate. Join hands with peo-ple
of the faith, reach out in hope to all who live.

Choose life, choose love – the hour is late!
Say 'yes' to Christ and 'no' to fate.
Join hands with people of the faith,
reach out in hope to all who live.

2 In seeking space and life for each,
we need to practise what we preach,
to turn into creative deeds
the inner urges of our creeds.

3 With Christ-the-Least, renouncing power,
we face the challenge of this hour,
we rise against the death of earth,
the end of life, the end of birth.

4 The hour is late! Choose life, choose love,
with Christ into God's future move:
life to the full, the earth a feast,
through making, speaking, *being* peace!

Fred Kaan

4 A HYMN (ANOTHER ONE?) FOR CHRISTMAS

MARAZAN 9 10 9 10

Fred Kaan
harm. Peter Cutts

Give thanks to God for Word of Christ - mas, for Christ a -

-mong us, near as bread and wine; re - joice in won - der at this

small - ness that draws to - ge - ther all the cos - mic scene.

PYENOT HALL 9 10 9 10   Peter Cutts

Give thanks to God for Word of Christ-mas, for Christ a-mong us, near as bread and wine; re-joice in won-der at this small-ness that draws to-ge-ther all the cos-mic scene.

Give thanks to God for Word of Christmas,
for Christ among us, near as bread and wine;
rejoice in wonder at this smallness
that draws together all the cosmic scene.

2 Rejoice, be still, as love incarnate
is bred into our very blood and bone;
give thanks for being and becoming:
our past, our future, woven into one.

3 Give thanks to God for soul and body,
for seed and soil — the miracle of life;
rejoice in hope, conceived and given,
take love beyond the limits of belief.

4 Rejoice, reach out for peace and wholeness
by being fully of this time and earth.
Give thanks! In Christ, alive beside us,
our highest human-ness is brought to birth!

Fred Kaan

5 A HYMN FOR MOTHERING SUNDAY

PENHILL 87 87

Pamela Ward

God of Eve and God of Ma-ry, God of love and mo-ther-earth,

thank you for the ones who with us shared their life and gave us birth.

English Traditional Melody
adapted R. Vaughan Williams

SUSSEX 87 87

God of Eve and God of Ma-ry, God of love and mo-ther-earth,

thank you for the ones who with us shared their life and gave us birth.

God of Eve and God of Mary,
God of love and mother-earth,
thank you for the ones who with us
shared their life and gave us birth.

2 As you came to earth in Jesus,
so you come to us today;
you are present in the caring
that prepares us for life's way.

3 Thank you, that the Church, our Mother,
gives us bread and fills our cup,
and the comfort of the Spirit
warms our hearts and lifts us up.

4 Thank you for belonging, shelter,
bonds of friendship, ties of blood,
and for those who have no children,
yet are parents under God.

5 God of Eve and God of Mary,
Christ our Brother, human Son,
Spirit, caring like a Mother,
take our love and make us one!

Fred Kaan

6 A HYMN FOR PEOPLE SEEKING RELEASE FROM BROKEN RELATIONSHIPS AND FORGIVENESS FOR HAVING FAILED OTHERS

LAUS DEO (REDHEAD No.46) 87 87   R. Redhead

God! When hu - man bonds are __ bro - ken

and we lack the love or __ skill to re - store the

hope of heal - ing, give us grace and make us still.

God! When human bonds are broken
and we lack the love or skill
to restore the hope of healing,
give us grace and make us still.

2 Through that stillness, with your Spirit
come into our world of stress,
for the sake of Christ forgiving
all the failures we confess.

3 You in us are bruised and broken:
hear us as we seek release
from the pain of earlier living;
set us free and grant us peace.

4 Send us, God of new beginnings,
humbly hopeful into life.
Use us as a means of blessing:
make us stronger, give us faith.

5 Give us faith to be more faithful,
give us hope to be more true,
give us love to go on learning:
God! Encourage and renew!

Fred Kaan

7 A HYMN ON PASSIONATE PEACE-MAKING

WOODLANDS 10 10 10 10   Walter Greatorex

Lord, while the world with war and ha-tred burns,

we skim a – cross the sur-face of con – cerns

and though we pray for peace in Je – sus' name,

Lord, while the world with war and hatred burns,
we skim across the surface of concerns
and though we pray for peace in Jesus' name,
we lack so often urgency and shame.

2 Forgive your church its calm pursuit of peace,
from idleness of will our lives release;
for justice make us hungry, help us reach
with all our passion for the good of each.

3 Speak through our voice protesting at the skill
and science used to cripple and to kill.
Weep with our tears, as every weapon made
robs yet another child of human bread.

4 Cause anger, Lord, to rise within our soul,
as all that you intended to be whole
and full of joy is trampled underfoot
by dint of war-machine and soldier's boot.

5 Teach us to use this anger and our will
to sweep away the forces out to kill
the life, the love you had of old in mind;
we pledge our word: we are *for* humankind!

Fred Kaan

8 HANDS SHAPED LIKE A CRADLE

ACH GOTT UND HERR 87 87

harm. J. S. Bach

Put peace in - to each — o - ther's hands

and like _ a trea-sure _ hold __ it, pro - tect it like a

can - dle _ flame, with ten-der-ness _ en - fold ___ it.

Alternative tune: St. Columba

Put peace into each other's hands
and like a treasure hold it,
protect it like a candle-flame,
with tenderness enfold it.

2 Put peace into each other's hands
with loving expectation;
be gentle in your words and ways,
in touch with God's creation.

3 Put peace into each other's hands,
like bread we break for sharing;
look people warmly in the eye:
our life is meant for caring.

4 As at communion, shape your hands
into a waiting cradle;
the gift of Christ receive, revere,
united round the table.

5 Put Christ into each other's hands,
he is love's deepest measure;
in love make peace, give peace a chance
and share it like a treasure.

Fred Kaan

9 'WHO SINGS, PRAYS TWICE' *St Augustine*

OLWEN 668 668 D

Welsh Carol Melody arr. Erik Routley

'Qui can-tat, bis— o-rat': our words borne on mu-sic as-

-cend on the— lad-der of prayer. We scale with our—

sing-ing and rise up in cho-rus for— life that is—

no-ble and fair. Once sing-ing, we're pray-ing and—
Then|teach us, Cre-a-tor, to

dou-ble our— long-ing for friend-ship to-ge-ther on—
see you be-side us; you are our be-gin-ning, our—

Put peace into each other's hands
and like a treasure hold it,
protect it like a candle-flame,
with tenderness enfold it.

2 Put peace into each other's hands
with loving expectation;
be gentle in your words and ways,
in touch with God's creation.

3 Put peace into each other's hands,
like bread we break for sharing;
look people warmly in the eye:
our life is meant for caring.

4 As at communion, shape your hands
into a waiting cradle;
the gift of Christ receive, revere,
united round the table.

5 Put Christ into each other's hands,
he is love's deepest measure;
in love make peace, give peace a chance
and share it like a treasure.

Fred Kaan

9 'WHO SINGS, PRAYS TWICE' *St Augustine*

OLWEN 668 668 D

Welsh Carol Melody arr. Erik Routley

'Qui can-tat, bis— o-rat': our words borne on mu-sic as-

-cend on the— lad-der of prayer. We scale with our—

sing-ing and rise up in cho-rus for— life that is—

no-ble and fair. Once sing-ing, we're pray-ing and—
Then|teach us, Cre - a - tor, to

dou-ble our— long-ing for friend-ship to-ge-ther on—
see you be - side us; you are our be - gin-ning, our—

earth; we pray for the_ one - ness of men, wo - men,
end. Be with us in_ be - ing and in our be -

child - ren in search of their_ call - ing and worth.
-com - ing, God, cos - mic, yet close as a friend.

'Qui cantat, bis orat':
our words borne on music
ascend on the ladder of prayer.
We scale with our singing
and rise up in chorus
for life that is noble and fair.
Once singing, we're praying
and double our longing
for friendship together on earth;
we pray for the one-ness
of men, women, children
in search of their calling and worth.
Then teach us, Creator,
to see you beside us;
you are our beginning, our end.
Be with us in being
and in our becoming,
God, cosmic, yet close as a friend.

Fred Kaan

USA © 1989 by Hope Publishing Company, Carol Stream, IL 60188
World outside USA © Oxford University Press 1989

10 A HYMN ON MUSIC AND PRAISE

CHADWICK 99 99

Peter Cutts

Thank you, God, ___ that long be - fore all time ___
your great Spi - - rit, source of rea - son, rhyme, ___
set the tone for all that came to be,
changed dis - or - der in - to har - mo - ny.

Thank you, God, that long before all time
your great Spirit, source of reason, rhyme,
set the tone for all that came to be,
changed disorder into harmony.

2 Thank you for the prelude of your Word,
  – theme alluding to the final chord –
  for the fugue of each creative deed,
  for the score you give your world to read.

3 Thank you for the way creation sings,
  for the beauty of the truth that rings,
  for the keys in which we learn to play,
  for the counterpoint of night and day.

4 Thank you, God, for melody and mirth,
  for the hymns that circle all the earth.
  Thank you for cantata, reggae, jazz,
  songs of protest, symphonies of praise.

5 Thank you for a universe of sound,
  for the lure of rhythm, dance and round.
  Thank you for the life and lead of Christ:
  Come, Lord Jesus, take us to the feast!

Fred Kaan

11 ROUND-TABLE CHURCH

HOLLY LANE 76 77 76   Pamela Ward

The church is like a ta – ble, a ta - ble that is round. It has no sides or cor – ners, no first or last, no ho – nours; here peo - ple are in one – ness and love to - ge - ther bound.

The church is like a table,
a table that is round.
It has no sides or corners,
no first or last, no honours;
here people are in one-ness
and love together bound.

2 The church is like a table
set in an open house;
no protocol for seating,
a symbol of inviting,
of sharing, drinking, eating;
an end to them and us.

3 The church is like a table,
a table for a feast
to celebrate the healing
of all excluded-feeling,
(while Christ is serving, kneeling,
a towel round his waist).

4 The church is like a table,
where every head is crowned.
As guests of God created,
all are to each related;
the whole world is awaited
to make the circle round.

Fred Kaan

CHRISTUS DER IST MEIN LEBEN 76 76   M. Vulpius

To live at peace with o - thers, we___

have to___ leave them room to love us or re -

-ject ___ us, to walk___ a - way or come.

USA Words © 1989 by Hope Publishing Company, Carol Stream, IL 60188
World outside USA Words © Oxford University Press 1989

To live at peace with others,
we have to leave them room
to love us or reject us us,
to walk away or come.

2 To live at peace with others,
we have to give them space
to question, challenge, know us,
oppose us to our face.

3 To live at peace with others,
we have to set them free
to choose to differ from us
in all they need to be.

4 Then, Prince of Peace among us,
come, help us to explore
new ways of love and living
as means to banish war,

5 and give us grace and wisdom,
while trying to be friends,
to use our inmost anger
for your creative ends.

Fred Kaan

13 A HYMN ON EMPTY HANDS

EL ESCORIAL 11 10 11 10   Rieke Boerma

We come with emp-ty hands, in-tent on shar-ing, our

needs, our wealth – but more! all that we *are*. We

meet as part-ners for each o-ther car-ing, at

one with peo-ple lack-ing voice or power.

STRENGTH AND STAY 11 10 11 10   J. B. Dykes

We come with emp-ty hands, in-tent on shar-ing,

We come with empty hands, intent on sharing.
our needs, our wealth — but more! all that we *are*.
We meet as partners for each other caring,
at one with people lacking voice or power.

2 We come to learn the courage of creating
a world of justice, hope and human worth,
to practise skills and secrets of translating
our words of faith into the life of earth.

3 We would be true in sharing of resources,
—in freedom eager to receive and give—
be open to the Spirit's gifts and forces,
be broken for the world in which we live.

4 Then widen, God, our vision and vocation,
our joy at what in Christ you showed and gave;
as still you share your Self with all creation,
help us respond with all we are and have.

Fred Kaan

USA Words © 1989 by Hope Publishing Company, Carol Stream, IL 60188
World outside USA Words © Oxford University Press 1989

14 AN ANTHEM FOR A BIRTHDAY CHURCH

SALVE FESTA DIES Irregular

R. Vaughan Williams

Refrain

Wel-come, day of the Lord! Glad day of rememb'ring and wor - ship,

day to give thanks for the past, fac-ing the fu - ture with hope.

Verses 1 and 3

Praise to the Spi-rit of God at work in the thrust of cre - a - tion,

D.C.

life - giv-ing Breath who cau-ses peo-ple to stand on their feet.

Praise to the Christ who in-spired us to cou-rage in com - ing to-ge-ther,

D.C.

calls us to reach out for peace, plant-ing our foot - prints of faith. ___

Welcome, day of the Lord!
Glad day of rememb'ring and worship,
day to give thanks for the past,
facing the future with hope.

1 Praise to the Spirit of God
  at work in the thrust of creation,
  life-giving Breath who causes
  people to stand on their feet.

2 Praise to the Christ who inspired
  us to courage in coming together,
  calls us to reach out for peace,
  planting our footprints of faith.

3 Praise to our Covenant-God
  who warns us against backward-looking,
  now as we renew obedience,
  serving as agents of change.

4 Praise to the Father, the Son,
  to the Spirit who guides and unsettles,
  giving us life to the full,
  sharing our journey of love.

Fred Kaan

15 A HYMN FOR AN ANNIVERSARY

LAUDATE DOMINUM 10 10 11 11

C. H. H. Parry

We pause to give thanks and fo-cus our thought on

how far our God his peo-ple has brought.

We pause for af-fir-ming our 'yes' to his call, pur-

-su-ing his fu-ture: life's full-ness for all.

Alternative tune: Hanover

'Let us practise today the destiny of tomorrow'
Jürgen Moltmann

We pause to give thanks
and focus our thought
on how far our God
his people has brought.
We pause for affirming
our 'yes' to his call,
pursuing his future:
life's fullness for all.

2 The future is here
as Christ sets us free;
we reach out in hope
for all that will be.
We go where he leads us,
to time's furthest ends,
to share in his mission
as partners and friends.

3 We rise and we risk
the course he has set,
to care for our world,
a world of 'not yet';
at one in the Spirit,
we follow Christ's way
and put into practice
God's future today.

4 Creator of worlds,
our Future and Source,
all that we are now,
or will be, is yours.
Enlarge our devotion,
as humbly we vow
to bring your tomorrow
to bear on our *now!*

Fred Kaan

16 A HYMN ON NOT GIVING UP

STUTTGART 87 87

Melody by C. F. Witt

Were the world to end tomorrow, would we plant a tree today? Would we till the soil of loving, kneel to work and rise to pray?

Were the world to end tomorrow,
would we plant a tree today?
Would we till the soil of loving,
kneel to work and rise to pray?

2 Dare we try to give an answer,
reaching out in fragile hope;
touching lives with words of Easter,
break a loaf and share a cup?

3 Born into the brittle morning
of that final earthy day,
we would be intent on seeing
Christ in others on our way.

4 Pray that at the end of living,
of philosophies and creeds,
God will find his people busy
planting trees and sowing seeds.

Fred Kaan

17 A HYMN OUT OF THE DEPTHS

ST LEONARD 87 87 77

Melody by J. C. Bach

When, O God, our faith is tested and our hope is un-der-mined,

when our love of li-ving shri-vels and we feel be-reft and drained,

then we turn to you and cry for your an-swer to our 'why?'

Alternative tune: All Saints

When, O God, our faith is tested
and our hope is undermined,
when our love of living shrivels
and we feel bereft and drained,
    then we turn to you and cry
    for your answer to our 'why?'

2 With emotions taut to breaking,
hearts with hurt and havoc frayed,
reason by remorse diminished,
souls distraught as if betrayed,
    God of bleakness and abyss,
    why have you forsaken us?

3 As we question and accuse you
out of depths of being tried,
could it be, God! that in weakness
you yourself are crucified?
    Are you with us in our grief?
    Help us in our unbelief!

Fred Kaan

18 A HYMN ON PEACE STEWARDSHIP

ANSTRUTHER 11 10 11 10   Peter Cutts

You gave us, God, this earth to hold and che-rish,
to praise you in our use of time and space,
but, blin-ded by our greed, the peo-ple pe-rish;
we throw your gift of free-dom in your face.

You gave us, God, this earth to hold and cherish,
to praise you in our use of time and space,
but, blinded by our greed, the people perish;
we throw your gift of freedom in your face.

2 As with un-human madness we offend you
and with our bombs and bullets break your heart,
with money made from conflict we un-friend you,
we tear with prejudice your world apart.

3 We glorify the sin of pointless dying
through mines and missiles poised in soil and sea,
perfect the curse of daily crucifying
your Son, ourselves, each other, you and me.

4 Raise up among us prophets who will guide us
with action, speech and silence to your peace,
where fear, mistrust no longer will divide us,
where hurt is healed and captives are released.

5 Renew in us our faith and trust in Jesus,
the Man, the Woman in your image made,
and speak again your Word that truly frees us
to beat our sword into a simple spade.

Fred Kaan

19a

A house has different rooms,
we go through many doors;
the church is like a house
and all its space is ours.

The church is like a home,
a roof to shelter all:
together or apart,
the toddlers and the tall.

We're here in Jesus' name,
who said that he would be
among us in the crowd,
or met as two or three.

Suggested tune: St Cecilia

19b

Although we go our separate ways
to listen, learn and teach,
keep us together, Lord, and share
your love with all and each;

and let us hear the news of Christ
so that, when worship's done,
we may be full of Easter-life,
then go and pass it on!

Suggested tune: St Bernard

19c

All Upstairs? Downstairs? God is there!
God is here and everywhere.
In the church and in the street,
God is there for all to meet.

Met in circles, large and small
we keep listening to God's call,
keen in love and faith to grow,
more of Christ-for-life to know.

Grown-ups As you leave us, so we pray:
'Peace be with you on your way.'
Children 'Peace with you, who stay behind,
God be in your heart and mind.'

Suggested tune: Vienna

19d

Wherever we may go,
God is already there;
we follow where he leads
and what he is, we share.

Before we came to church,
God longed for us to come;
his love invites us out,
to be with him at home.

Wherever we may be,
our God has been before,
and Jesus is the key
to open every door.

Unite us, Lord, as now
we go our separate ways
and let your Spirit guide
each one who goes or stays.

Suggested tunes: Quam Dilecta *or* St Cecilia

NOTES

1 A TIME-WARP HYMN

This text was written for Central Church, Swindon, in January 1987, when we began a series of evening services centered around the so-called 'I AM' sayings of Jesus recorded in John's gospel. Our Lord's words: Before Abraham was, I am (John 8:58) have always particularly intrigued me, and so this time-warp hymn came about. The tune KAIROS was composed especially for it by John Garside, the church's staffing officer who is also one of its organists.

2 A HYMN TO THE TUNE OF 'TEA FOR TWO' — WHY NOT?

The challenge to write this text was given to me over breakfast at the 1985 General Assembly of the United Reformed Church, held in Southend-on-Sea. A fellow-delegate asked me how long it would take for me to write a text — say to the tune of 'Tea for Two', which drew from me the promise that I would have something ready that same day. As it happened, a 'first edition' had come about by coffee time that morning. I tidied it up three months later during a not altogether riveting session of the Prague Peace Conference.

3 A HYMN ON CHOOSING LIFE

In July 1985 I was invited as a special guest to attend the Sixth All Christian Peace Conference in Prague, Czechoslovakia. The conference theme, Choose Life — The Hour Is Late, sparked off this text early on during the proceedings; we sang it later in a plenary session to the tune EISENACH.

4 A HYMN (ANOTHER ONE?) FOR CHRISTMAS

Although conscious of the fact that there is already a vast store of Christmas hymns and carols from which to draw, I did one day during Advent 1985 sit down to try and draw together the smallness and the cosmic, and give thanks for the interwovenness of Christ's and our humanity.

5 A HYMN FOR MOTHERING SUNDAY

This was written early in 1987 for Penhill United Reformed Church, the small housing estate congregation in North Swindon which I served as a part-time minister. Pamela Ward, URC minister in Erdington, Birmingham, composed the tune PENHILL for it. The hymn was included in the seven runners-up in a hymn-writing competition organised by BBC television later that year, and is incorporated in *New Songs of Praise 4* published by Oxford University Press (see also note on hymn no.8).

6 A HYMN FOR PEOPLE SEEKING RELEASE FROM BROKEN RE-LATIONSHIPS AND FORGIVENESS FOR HAVING FAILED OTHERS

Triggered off, in part, by an experimental order of service devised by URC minister John Johansen-Berg in 1977 "to help individuals or couples who have been given a legal divorce, but desire to seek release from vows made before God, so that they may feel free to make a new beginning". The hymn, written in 1988, obviously has wider applications and may be helpful in any situation where human relationships have broken down.

7 A HYMN ON PASSIONATE PEACE-MAKING

This hymn came about after reading a poem entitled *November 11* by Margaret Allen, of Glenridding in the Lake District. The poem was part of a larger handwritten collection of peace texts discovered in a small exercise book after her death in 1985. My own text originally had two additional preceding verses closely based on Margaret's poem, but these I subsequently dropped. I include them here for the record:

> This is the day of marching and commands,
> of high-and-mighty, clergy, crowds and bands
> assembled for the year's assertive scene
> (with sackcloth, ashes, nowhere to be seen)

> Encased in brass, with patriotic tone,
> we sing: sufficient is thine arm alone,
> yet put our self-importance on parade
> with vanity of medals, stars and braid.

8 HANDS SHAPED LIKE A CRADLE

In many Christian traditions where people go forward to the altar rail for Holy Communion, they often shape their two hands like a cradle in order to receive the bread. Beth-lehem (Hebrew meaning 'house of bread') did not really fulfil its name until Jesus (the Bread of life) was laid in the manger! This communion hymn, written in August 1987, was inspired by this observed 'liturgical gesture'.

The text progresses from a treasure *held* in verse 1 to a treasure *being handed on* in verse 5. The original choice of tune (ACH, GOTT UND HERR) was motivated by the fact that it is used for the well-known post-communion hymn from the liturgy of Malabar: Strengthen for service, Lord, the hands that holy things have taken; the idea being that both hymns might be sung to the same tune, before and after the sacrament.

The hymn was one of the eight winning entries in a hymn-writing competition for the 1988 Songs of Praise Festival of New Hymns, organised by BBC television. The text, together with no.5 in this collection, was published by Oxford University Press in the Festival booklet: *New Songs of Praise 4*.

9 WHO SINGS, PRAYS TWICE

I have often wondered what Saint Augustine actually meant when he said: Qui cantat bis orat (the person who sings, prays twice). Maybe he meant that music is brought in to strengthen and emphasise the words; or that singers use − and thus repeat − words and music already written and composed by others; or that in worship we normally sing alongside one another. However he meant it, singing is an intensified and corporate act of approaching God.

This hymn was written on the last Sunday of the Christian Year, 1988, to the Welsh tune OLWEN.

10 A HYMN ON MUSIC AND PRAISE

I was commissioned to write a hymn for Perrymount Methodist Church in Haywards Heath, Sussex, to mark its choir's anniversary on 28 April 1985, when I was visiting preacher for the occasion. Kathleen Johnson, the church's choirmistress, wrote a tune specially for it, at the same time also composing a full choir anthem setting, which was performed on the day.

The hymn appears here to another melody (CHADWICK) composed for it by Peter Cutts (b. 1937); it was in this version that we submitted it in a hymn-writing contest by the American Guild of Organists in 1986.

11 ROUND-TABLE CHURCH

This text only just made it into my book *The Hymn-Texts of Fred Kaan* (1985) in which it was printed in hand-written facsimile form. The success of the hymn and its quick world-wide spread owes much to the tune HOLLY LANE composed for it by Pamela Ward (see note on hymn no.5). It is here in this collection that this melody is officially published for the first time. It is especially in circles related to the Council for World Mission that the hymn has found such a strong echo, because its imagery is felt to illustrate the basic principles of equal partnership and sharing that underlie CWM's formation and work.

The hymn owes its inspiration to a poem by Chuck Lathrop, a former Maryknoll missioner in the Appalachian Mountains, USA, and now living in Ireland.

I wrote the hymn on the 7.40 train from Coventry to London on 14 December 1984.

12 HATING THE SIN WHILE TRYING TO LOVE THE SINNER

Written for the Central Church, Swindon, for the sixth Sunday after Christmas (1 February 1987), to go with the sermon I preached on the theme appointed for the day: Christ the Friend of sinners, based on the Gospel reading: Mark 2:13–17. We sang it to CHRISTUS DER IST MEIN LEBEN.

13 A HYMN ON EMPTY HANDS

I was commisioned to write a conference hymn for the World Council of Churches consultation on Ecumenical Sharing of Resources, held in El Escorial, Spain, in October 1987. The hymn was soon translated into French, German, Spanish, and Dutch, and sung to a tune especially written for it by Rieke Boerma, a Dutch composer living in Switzerland. Given the theme of the consultation (Empty Hands – An Agenda For the Churches), the hymn may also be found applicable during One World Week, observed annually in the UK around the third week in October (thus incorporating United Nations Day on the 24th).

14 AN ANTHEM FOR A BIRTHDAY CHURCH

Challenged to write something for the tenth anniversary of Central Church, Swindon, (21–28 February 1988) to Ralph Vaughan Williams' SALVE FESTA DIES, this is the text I came up with. Central Church is an ecumenical congregation made up of four different denominations (Anglican, Baptist, Methodist and United Reformed). A record of the first ten years of ecumenical journeying together was published under the title *Footprints of Faith*.

15 A HYMN FOR AN ANNIVERSARY

In 1987 the Council for World Mission celebrated its tenth anniversary and I was commissioned to write a hymn to mark the occasion. The hymn was given its official première at a thanksgiving service in Hong Kong on 9 July 1987, when it was sung in English and Cantonese (translated by Dr Hayward Wong). The theme of the anniversary, 'God's Future Today' and of this hymn was inspired by Jürgen Moltmann's line: Let us practise today the destiny of tomorrow; the text is dedicated to him. The hymn was also used in CWM member churches – 28 churches in 21 countries – on the Sunday following the Hong Kong celebration.

The hymn is also offered for use in local and other anniversary events.

16 A HYMN ON NOT GIVING UP

Martin Luther was once asked how he would spend today if he knew that the world was coming to an end tomorrow. He is reported to have replied that he would plant an apple tree. It was this question and answer that suggested the theme for an elders' retreat I was invited to lead at St Ninian's United Reformed Church, Solihull, Birmingham, on 27 April 1980: Witness with a sense of urgency.

It was not until early 1986, though, that I wrote this text, which I used as an illustration in my inaugural sermon at Central Church, Swindon, but which I have dedicated to St Ninian's. Like hymn no. 10, I wrote it on the 7.40 Coventry to London train.

17 A HYMN OUT OF THE DEPTHS

My strong emotional involvement with a young couple who tragically lost their 15-months old son in a drowning accident in Dubai, led me to write this text, which I was able to share with the mourners at the boy's funeral. It was written in August 1986, with the tune ST LEONARD in mind.

18 A HYMN ON PEACE STEWARDSHIP

This hymn was written for the 1986 'Bread not Bombs' week, an event which is organised annually by CAAT, the Campaign Against the Arms Trade. Suggested tune: ZU MEINEM HERRN

19 FOUR HYMNS FOR WHEN THE JUNIOR CHURCH IS ABOUT TO 'LEAVE'

A batch of four short hymns to be sung in morning worship just prior to Junior Church (Sunday School) members and leaders 'leaving' family worship in order to take up their own Christian education programme in groups. The texts were all written during the course of 1987, and are set to well-known tunes.